THE BIG BOOK OF PO[illegible]

AN EDUCATIONAL COUNTRY TRAVEL PICTURE BOOK FOR KIDS ABOUT HISTORY, DESTINATION PLACES, ANIMALS AND MANY MORE

Portugal is a country in Europe located on the Iberian Peninsula.

What is the national sport of the Portugal ?

Football (soccer) is considered the national sport of Portugal .

What is the official name of the Portugal ?

Portugal's official name is the Portuguese Republic.

What is the national flower of the Portugal ?

The national flower of Portugal is carnation.

What is the national tree of the Portugal ?

Portugal's national tree is the cork oak.

What is the national fruit of the Portugal ?

The national fruit of Portugal is cherry.

What is the national food of the Portugal ?

The national food of Portugal is bacalhau, which is salted codfish.

What is the national animal of the Portugal ?

An Iberian wolf

What is the national bird of the Portugal ?

The national bird of Portugal is the Galo de Barcelos, or Rooster of Barcelos.

The capital city of Portugal is Lisbon.

Portugal is known for its **beautiful beaches, stunning coastline, and sunny weather.**

BASIC PORTUGUESE WORDS AND SENTENCES WITH THEIR ENGLISH TRANSLATIONS:

- **Olá** - Hello
- **Bom dia** - Good morning
- **Boa tarde** - Good afternoon
- **Boa noite** - Good evening/night
- **Obrigado/a** - Thank you (male/female)
- **Sim** - Yes
- **Não** - No
- **Por favor** - Please
- **Desculpe** - Excuse me
- **Com licença** - Pardon me
- **Adeus** - Goodbye
- **Como está?** - How are you?
- **Estou bem, obrigado/a.** - I'm fine, thank you (male/female).
- **Qual é o seu nome?** - What is your name?
- **Meu nome é...** - My name is...
- **Onde fica...?** - Where is...?
- **Quanto custa?** - How much does it cost?
- **Eu não entendo.** - I don't understand.
- **Fala inglês?** - Do you speak English?
- **Eu falo um pouco de português.** - I speak a little Portuguese.
- **Por favor, repita**. - Please, repeat.
- **Socorro**! - Help!
- **Preciso de ajuda.** - I need help.
- Estou perdido/a. - I am lost (male/female).
- **Onde está o banheiro?** - Where is the bathroom?
- **Comida** - Food
- **Bebida** - Drink
- **Água** - Water
- **Café** - Coffee
- **Chá** - Tea
- **Pão** - Bread
- **Queijo** - Cheese
- **Carne** - Meat
- **Peixe** - Fish
- **Fruta** - Fruit
- **Verdura** - Vegetable
- **Casa** - House
- **Quarto** - Room
- **Banheiro** - Bathroom
- **Cozinha** - Kitchen
- **Escola** - School
- **Livro** - Book
- **Caneta** - Pen
- **Computador** - Computer
- **Telefone** - Telephone
- **Cidade** - City
- **Praia** - Beach
- **Montanha** - Mountain
- **Parque** - Park
- **Amigo/a** - Friend

The official language of Portugal is **Portuguese**.

Portugal is one of the oldest countries in Europe, with a history that goes back over 800 years.

The currency used in Portugal is the Euro.

Portugal is famous for its delicious food, including dishes like pastéis de nata (custard tarts) and bacalhau (salted codfish).

The Portuguese love to play and watch soccer, which is a very popular sport in the country.

Portugal is home to Cristiano Ronaldo, one of the greatest soccer players in the world.

The Portuguese are known for their traditional folk music called fado, which is often sung with emotion and sadness.

Portugal has a rich maritime history and was once a powerful seafaring nation.

The Portuguese explorer Vasco da Gama was the first person to sail from Europe to India, opening up a sea route to the East.

The longest bridge in Europe, Vasco da Gama Bridge, is located in Portugal.

The Portuguese are also known for their beautiful traditional tiles called azulejos, which can be seen on many buildings in the country.

Portugal has a variety of landscapes, including mountains, rolling hills, and fertile plains.

The Douro Valley in Portugal is famous for its vineyards and the production of Port wine.

The University of Coimbra in Portugal is one of the oldest universities in the world, founded in 1290.

The Tower of Belém in Lisbon is a UNESCO World Heritage site and a symbol of Portugal's maritime history.

Portugal has several beautiful castles and palaces, such as the Pena Palace in Sintra.

The Portuguese love to celebrate festivals and holidays, with colorful parades and traditional dances.

The Carnation Revolution in 1974 marked the end of a dictatorship in Portugal and the beginning of a democratic government.

Portugal is a member of the European Union and uses the Euro as its currency.

The westernmost point of Europe, Cabo da Roca, is located in Portugal.

The Portuguese language is spoken by more than 200 million people around the world.

Portugal is a popular tourist destination, attracting millions of visitors each year.

Portugal is known for its traditional handicrafts, such as pottery, embroidery, and cork products.

The Algarve region in Portugal is famous for its stunning beaches and golf resorts.

Lisbon has one of the oldest and largest fish markets in the world, called Mercado da Ribeira.

Portugal has several national parks and nature reserves, offering opportunities for hiking and wildlife observation.

The city of Porto is famous for its production of Port wine and its historic city center, a UNESCO World Heritage site.

- Portugal has a warm Mediterranean climate, with mild winters and hot summers.
- The national symbol of Portugal is the rooster, called the "Galo de Barcelos."
- Portugal is known for its traditional fishing villages, where you can find colorful boats and fresh seafood.
- The Portuguese love to drink coffee, and you can find small coffee shops called "cafés" all over the country.
- The traditional Portuguese houses are often painted in bright colors, such as yellow, blue, and pink.
- The cork oak tree is native to Portugal, and the country is the world's largest producer of cork.
- The Tagus River is the longest river in Portugal, running through the capital city of Lisbon.
- Portugal has a strong tradition of bullfighting, although it has become controversial in recent years.
- The city of Évora in Portugal is a UNESCO World Heritage site, known for its well-preserved Roman temple.
- Portugal is home to several beautiful islands, including Madeira and the Azores.
- The Vasco da Gama Tower in Lisbon is one of the tallest buildings in Portugal, offering panoramic views of the city.
- Portugal has a high literacy rate, with a strong emphasis on education.
- The Portuguese love to eat seafood, and dishes like grilled sardines and seafood rice are popular.
- Portugal has a rich cultural heritage, with influences from its former colonies, such as Brazil and Angola.
- The Portuguese are known for their warm and friendly hospitality towards visitors.
- Portugal is a popular destination for surfers, with world-class waves along its coastline.
- The Jerónimos Monastery in Lisbon is a UNESCO World Heritage site and a masterpiece of Manueline architecture.
- The Alentejo region in Portugal is known for its vast plains, vineyards, and traditional cork oak forests.
- Portugal is home to several unique species of birds, making it a great destination for birdwatching.
- Portuguese people love to celebrate St. Anthony's Day on June 13th, with street parties, music, and traditional food.

TEST YOUR KNOWLEDGE: 30 MULTIPLE-CHOICE QUESTIONS ABOUT PORTUGAL!

1	Which continent is Portugal located in? a) Asia b) Europe c) Africa d) South America
2	What is the capital city of Portugal? a) Barcelona b) Lisbon c) Madrid d) Porto
3	Which language is spoken in Portugal? a) English b) Spanish c) Portuguese d) French
4	Which currency is used in Portugal? a) Dollar b) Euro c) Pound d) Yen
5	Portugal is known for its beautiful: a) Mountains b) Deserts c) Beaches d) Rainforests
6	Who is one of the greatest soccer players from Portugal? a) Lionel Messi b) Cristiano Ronaldo c) Neymar Jr. d) Kylian Mbappé
7	What is the traditional folk music of Portugal called? a) Samba b) Fado c) Flamenco d) Tango
8	Portugal has a rich history in: a) Science b) Literature c) Maritime exploration d) Architecture
9	Who was the first person to sail from Europe to India, opening up a sea route to the East? a) Ferdinand Magellan b) Christopher Columbus c) Vasco da Gama d) James Cook
10	What are the traditional tiles called that can be seen on many buildings in Portugal? a) Azulejos b) Mosaics c) Stained glass d) Terracotta

11	What is the name of the famous wine region in Portugal known for its vineyards and the production of Port wine? a) Tuscany b) Bordeaux c) Douro Valley d) Napa Valley
12	Which city in Portugal is home to one of the oldest universities in the world? a) Coimbra b) Lisbon c) Porto d) Faro
13	Which landmark in Lisbon is a UNESCO World Heritage site and symbolizes Portugal's maritime history? a) Tower of Belém b) Eiffel Tower c) Colosseum d) Acropolis
14	Which region in Portugal is famous for its stunning castles and palaces? a) Porto b) Braga c) Coimbra d) Faro
15	What historical event marked the end of a dictatorship in Portugal and the beginning of a democratic government in 1974? a) Velvet Revolution b) Carnation Revolution c) French Revolution d) American Revolution
16	Which organization is Portugal a member of? a) United Nations b) NATO c) European Union d) OPEC
17	Which point in Portugal is the westernmost point of Europe? a) Gibraltar b) Cape Horn c) Cabo da Roca d) Cape of Good Hope
18	How many people speak Portuguese worldwide? a) More than 100 million b) More than 200 million c) More than 300 million d) More than 500 million
19	What is Portugal known for as a popular tourist destination? a) Ancient pyramids b) Volcanic eruptions c) Stunning beaches d) Snow-capped mountains
20	Which bridge located in Portugal is the longest in Europe? a) Golden Gate Bridge b) Vasco da Gama Bridge c) Tower Bridge d) Sydney Harbour Bridge

21	Which traditional Portuguese handicraft is made from the bark of cork oak trees?) Pottery b) Embroidery c) Cork products d) Woodcarving
22	Which region in Portugal is famous for its stunning beaches and golf resorts? a) Algarve b) Douro Valley c) Azores d) Madeira
23	Which city in Portugal has one of the oldest and largest fish markets in the world? a) Lisbon b) Porto c) Faro d) Coimbra
24	What does UNESCO stand for? a) United Nations Educational, Scientific and Cultural Organization b) United Nations Economic and Social Council c) United Nations Environmental and Sustainability Council d) United Nations European Science Organization
25	Which Portuguese river runs through the capital city of Lisbon? a) Tagus River b) Nile River c) Danube River d) Amazon River
26	Which animal is the national symbol of Portugal? a) Lion b) Rooster c) Eagle d) Dolphin
27	What can you find in traditional Portuguese fishing villages? a) Colorful boats and fresh seafood b) Ancient ruins c) Amusement parks d) Ski resorts
28	What are small coffee shops called in Portugal? a) Cafeterias b) Patisseries c) Cafés d) Tea houses
29	What colors are often used to paint traditional Portuguese houses? a) Red, green, and white b) Yellow, blue, and pink c) Black and white d) Orange and purple
30	What is the largest producer of cork in the world? a) Spain b) Italy c) France d) Portugal

ANSWERS KEY:

1. b) Europe
2. b) Lisbon
3. c) Portuguese
4. b) Euro
5. c) Beaches
6. b) Cristiano Ronaldo
7. b) Fado
8. c) Maritime exploration
9. c) Vasco da Gama
10. a) Azulejos
11. c) Douro Valley
12. a) Coimbra
13. a) Tower of Belém
14. c) Sintra
15. b) Carnation Revolution
16. c) European Union
17. c) Cabo da Roca
18. b) More than 200 million
19. c) Stunning beaches
20. b) Vasco da Gama Bridge
21. c) Cork products
22. a) Algarve
23. a) Lisbon
24. a) United Nations Educational, Scientific and Cultural Organization
25. a) Tagus River
26. b) Rooster
27. a) Colorful boats and fresh seafood
28. c) Cafés
29. b) Yellow, blue, and pink
30. d) Portugal

20 travel tips for visiting Portugal

1. Learn a few basic Portuguese phrases to help you communicate with locals.
2. Pack comfortable shoes as you'll be doing a lot of walking in Portugal's charming cities.
3. Try the local cuisine, including famous dishes like bacalhau (codfish) and pastel de nata (custard tart).
4. Explore Lisbon's historic neighborhoods, such as Alfama and Bairro Alto.
5. Visit Porto and sample its renowned port wine.
6. Take a leisurely stroll along the beautiful beaches of the Algarve region.
7. Don't forget to try the famous Portuguese custard tarts called pastéis de Belém in Lisbon.
8. Visit Sintra and explore its fairy tale-like castles and palaces.
9. Be prepared for changing weather conditions, as Portugal's climate can be unpredictable.
10. Take advantage of the extensive public transportation system, including trains and buses.
11. Respect the local customs and traditions, such as avoiding excessive noise in residential areas.
12. Visit the Douro Valley for stunning landscapes and vineyards.
13. Be cautious of pickpockets, especially in crowded tourist areas. Keep your belongings secure.
14. Try the local wines, including vinho verde and red wines from the Alentejo region.
15. Visit the Azores or Madeira islands for their natural beauty and outdoor activities.
16. Take a boat tour along the Ria Formosa Natural Park in the Algarve to see its diverse wildlife.
17. Enjoy a fado music performance, a traditional Portuguese music genre known for its heartfelt lyrics.
18. Visit Évora and explore its well-preserved Roman ruins and medieval architecture.
19. Take a day trip to the picturesque village of Óbidos, surrounded by medieval walls.
20. Enjoy the relaxed pace of life in Portugal and take time to savor the local culture and scenery.

general differences in rules and customs you may encounter in Portugal compared to other countries:

1. Driving: In Portugal, you drive on the right-hand side of the road. Additionally, some driving customs, such as giving way to vehicles on your right at roundabouts, may be different from other countries.
2. Tipping: While tipping is appreciated in Portugal, it is not as customary or expected as in some other countries. However, leaving a small tip (around 5-10%) at restaurants and for good service is common.
3. Meal times: Portuguese meal times may differ from those in other countries. Lunch is usually served between 12:30 pm and 2:30 pm, and dinner is typically served later, starting around 7:30 pm or 8:00 pm.
4. Greetings: In Portugal, it is customary to greet people with a handshake or two kisses on the cheek, even in more formal settings. This may vary compared to other countries where different forms of greetings are preferred.
5. Siesta time: Unlike some other Mediterranean countries, Portugal does not have a traditional siesta or afternoon break in businesses. Most shops and services operate continuously throughout the day.
6. Shopping hours: Many shops in Portugal close for a few hours in the afternoon, typically between 1:00 pm and 3:00 pm. It's good to plan accordingly and check the opening hours in advance.
7. Beach etiquette: Portugal has beautiful beaches, and it's important to follow certain rules and practices. For example, it is common to use a towel or beach mat instead of sitting directly on the sand, and some beaches have designated areas for nudism.
8. Smoking regulations: Portugal has implemented strict smoking regulations in recent years. Smoking is generally prohibited in enclosed public spaces, including restaurants and bars. Designated smoking areas may be available.

thank you
so much

Made in United States
North Haven, CT
20 May 2025